Grace Be With You

Benedictions from
Dale Ralph Davis

CHRISTIAN
FOCUS

Foreword by
Derek W. H. Thomas

Grace Be With You

Benedictions from Dale Ralph Davis

Afterword by
Sinclair B. Ferguson

Scripture quotations are from *The Holy Bible, English Standard Version*, copyright © 2001 by Crossway Bibles, a publishing ministry of Good News Publishers. Used by permission. All rights reserved. ESV Text Edition: 2011.

Copyright © Dale Ralph Davis 2018

ISBN 978-1-5271-0294-1

First published in 2018
This new edition published in 2019
by
Christian Focus Publications, Ltd
Geanies House, Fearn,
Ross-shire, IV20 1TW, Scotland
www.christianfocus.com

Cover and internal design by Daniel van Straaten

Printed by Bell and Bain, Glasgow

Contents

Foreword

In the summer of 2013, upon the retirement of Dr. Sinclair Ferguson as the Senior Minister of First Presbyterian Church, Columbia, I received a call to succeed him. For the previous two years, I had been 'the evening preacher.' First Presbyterian Church was therefore accustomed to a 'different voice' in the evenings, and even though I had been the 'evening preacher' at First Presbyterian Church in Jackson, Mississippi, for sixteen years and a solo minister in Belfast for seventeen years (with a weekly evening service), I was prepared to preach both morning and evening at First Columbia. However, and for entirely selfish reasons, the prospect of a Sunday afternoon nap following two morning services appealed to me. To help lighten the load a little, I asked my long-time friend, Dr. Dale Ralph Davis (aka, Ralph) to preach on four Sunday evenings in the Fall of 2013. Having retired from full-time ministry for a few years, he readily agreed, despite the six hour journey from where he and his wife, Barbara, then lived. It was immediately apparent after the first Sunday that the dear members of First Presbyterian were eager to hear more. The very next day, on Monday morning, I sent him an email asking if there was even the remotest possibility that he and Barbara would consider moving to Columbia and becoming the evening preacher. I never once thought that he would respond within the hour with a promise that he and Barbara would pray about it and give me an answer. Within days, the answer was 'yes'!

And so, for the last four and a half years, we have been privileged to sit and listen to expositions of Old Testament narrative passages that, quite simply, have taken us to the very throne room of Almighty God. I doubt there exists a pulpit in the world that could match the depth of exegesis or the pointed applications we have heard. Often reading and translating in the pulpit from the Hebrew text, we have been brought to tears by the singular grace of God and made to laugh out loud at our folly and stupidity. In the course of over four years we have learned a great deal about his family, his love of baseball, his fondness for ice cream and his ever-patient wife. We have watched him cope with grief in the death of a grandchild, and his evident care for the souls of others. It has been a moment in time, a season that we will never forget. And we are grateful beyond words for the ministry of the Word we were privileged to hear.

What stands out the most about these Sunday evening worship services were Dr. Davis's benedictions that concluded each service. For most of my life as a minister, I have stuck almost exclusively to a half dozen benedictions found in Scripture and identified as such. Ralph made up his own, often taking some verses from the passage he was preaching and turning them into a benediction. It was not only *what* he said, but *how* he said it.

Benedictions are gospel words. They remind us at the end of the service that we receive the blessings of God's covenant *because Christ received its curses*. After every service of worship, we conclude with a reminder that, as Christians, we live under the shade of the Almighty, taking refuge beneath His wings because, wonder of wonders, we are free from the condemnation of sin. And in a manner that, for some of us at least, was altogether unique and refreshing, we came to anticipate the benediction as never before.

It seemed obvious that these benedictions must be shared with others, and to my great delight, William Mackenzie at Christian Focus Publications (a long-time friend of the Davis's) thought so, too. It is with a great sense of gratitude, therefore, that we offer this book to our beloved evening preacher, Dr. Ralph Davis, on the occasion of his retirement. A very thankful congregation will miss him greatly.

Derek W. H. Thomas
May 2018

I

The Lord answer you in the day of trouble. The name of the God of Jacob protect you. May He send you help from the sanctuary and give you support from Zion. Amen.

15th September '13

2

A nd may the God of peace Himself make you holy through and through. May your whole being, spirit, soul, and body be kept blameless at the coming of our Lord Jesus Christ. The One who calls you is faithful and He will accomplish it. Amen.

29th September '13

3

And now may the Lord, who is the strength of His people, be your Shepherd and carry you forever. Amen.

13th September '13

4

The God of peace will soon
crush Satan under your feet.
The grace of the Lord Jesus be
with you all. Amen.

20th October '13

5

Now a dying Savior's love,
a risen Savior's joy, an
ascended Savior's power, and
a returning Savior's hope, rest
upon your hearts and your homes.
Amen.

24th November '13

6

May the God and Father of our Lord Jesus Christ, the Father of mercies and the God of all comfort, comfort you in all your afflictions, so that you may be able to comfort those who are in any affliction, with the comfort with which you yourself have been comforted by God. Amen.

9th February '14

7

May the Lord of peace Himself, grant you peace at all times, under all circumstances. The Lord be with you all. Amen.

9th March '14

8

The God of hope fill you with all joy and peace in believing so that by the power of the Holy Spirit, you may overflow in hope. Amen.

16th March '14

9

You only have to suffer a little while. The God of all grace, who called you to eternal glory in Christ, will see that all is well again. He will confort, strengthen and support you. His power lasts forever and ever. Amen.

13th April '14

10

May the companionship of the man of sorrows and the power of the King of glory rest upon you this day and all your days. Amen.

20th April '14

II

Now the Lord, Maker of heaven and earth, the keeper of Israel and your keeper, keep your going out and your coming in from now on and for all time. Amen.

25th May '14

12

The Lord be the shelter above you, the tower around you, and the rock beneath you all your days until Jesus comes. Amen.

13th July '14

13

Now the God who is from everlasting to everlasting, who has loved you with an everlasting love and gives you everlasting life, now support you with the everlasting arms in these days and all the days until Jesus comes. Amen.

7th September '14

14

Now the Savior, who died and rose and who reigns, grant you joy in the midst of labor, peace in the midst of troubles, hope in the midst of despair, and faithfulness in the midst of temptation. Amen.

12th October '14

15

Now the God, who hears your cries and listens to your prayers, be the shelter above you, the tower around you, the rock beneath you this day and all the days until Jesus comes. Amen.

26th October '14

16

Now the companionship of the man of sorrows, the power of the King of glory, rest upon you all. Amen.

9th November '14

17

Congregation of the Lord Jesus Christ, in all your troubles and darkness, remember what you are and have. You have been loved with an everlasting love. You are supported by everlasting arms. You are recipients of everlasting life and heirs of an everlasting kingdom, all sealed and made sure by the blood of an everlasting covenant. Amen.

23rd November '14

18

Now the Savior who died,
who lives and who reigns,
grant you joy in labor, peace in
troubles, hope in despair, and
faithfulness in temptation. Amen.

7th December '14

19

Now the Father, who loved you before the foundation of the world, the Son who set you free and made you His slave, and the Counselor who stands by you forever, give you ears to hear Him, hearts that crave Him, lives that reflect Him. Amen.

18th January '15

20

Now the Father who chose you, the Son who bought you, and the Spirit who dwells in you, go before you in your darkness, stand beside you in your fears and hold you up in your sorrows until Jesus comes. Amen.

22nd February '15

21

Now the God whose affection never cools, whose attentions never wavers, whose arm never relaxes, and whose grace never fails, rescue you from every evil attack and bring you safely to His heavenly kingdom. Amen.

5th April '15

22

The Father who chose you,
the Son who bought you,
and the Spirit who teaches you,
make goodness and mercy pursue
you all the days of your life and
preserve your life, though you
walk in the midst of trouble.
Amen.

26th April '15

23

Now Yahweh, Maker of heaven and earth, the keeper of Israel, your keeper, go before you in your darkness, stand beside you in your fears, and hold you up in your sorrows until Jesus comes. Amen.

17th May '15

24

Now may the God who never abandons you and never lets go of you, go before you in your darkness, stand beside you in your fears, make you faithful in your temptations until Jesus comes. Amen.

28th June '15

25

Oh may this bounteous God through all your life be near you, with ever joyful hearts and blessed peace to cheer you; and keep you in His grace, and guide you when perplexed, and free you from all ills in this world and the next. Amen.[1]

12th July '15

---

1 Adapted from Martin Rinkhart's hymn, 'Now Thank We All our God'.

26

Now the eternal God who is your refuge, be a rock that is beneath you, the tower that is around you, the shelter that is above you this day and all the days until Jesus comes. Amen.

26th July '15

27

Now the Father who chose you, the Son that bought you, the Spirit who dwells in you, go before you in your darkness, stand beside you in your fears, hold you up in your sorrows, until Jesus comes. Amen.

29th November '15

28

As the mountains surround Jerusalem, so may the Lord surround you, His people, from this time on and forever. Amen.

6th December '15

29

Now may the Lord, who is merciful and gracious, slow to anger, and rich in steadfast love and mercy, keep you from despair in all your troubles and keep you from idolatry in all your joys. Amen.

10th January '16

30

And now the Lord who has loved you with an everlasting love, support you all your days with the everlasting arms, until the day when the Lord binds up the brokenness of His people, and heals the wounds inflicted by His blow. Amen.

17th January '16

31

Now the Savior who died, who rose, and who reigns, grant you joy in the midst of labor, peace in the midst of troubles, hope in the midst of despair, and faithfulness in the midst of temptation. Amen.

24th January '16

32

Now may God be your exceeding joy, Christ your unfailing hope, and the Spirit your unfailing comforter, in all your worship and work and troubles until Jesus comes. Amen.

7th February '16

33

May the Lord hide you in His shelter in the day of trouble, conceal you under the cover of His tent, may He set you high upon a rock. Amen.

21st February '16

34

Now the God who is mighty,
the Lamb who is worthy,
and the Spirit who is near, fortify
you to live faithfully in these days
and all the days until Jesus comes.
Amen.

6th March '16

35

Now may the Shepherd who laid down His life for the sheep restore your soul, lead you in right paths, walk beside you in the dark valley, and bring you safely home to the home of the Lord forever more. Amen.

10th April '16

36

And now hear what Yahweh says,
The One who created you, Oh Jacob,
the One who formed you, Oh Israel:
'Do not be afraid, for I have redeemed
you, I have called you by name. You are
mine. When you pass through the waters,
I will be with you. And through the
rivers, they will not wash you away. When
you walk through fire, you will not be
scorched, and the flame will not burn you.
For I am Yahweh, your God, the holy One
of Israel, your Savior.' Amen.

22nd May '16

37

Now the God who has loved you with an everlasting love and has brought you into the bonds of an everlasting covenant, support you all the days with everlasting arms until the day when He places everlasting joy upon your heads. Amen.

12th June '16

38

Now the God of hope, fill you with all joy and peace in believing, so that by the power of the Holy Spirit you may overflow in hope. Amen.

19th June '16

39

Flock of the Lord Jesus Christ: May the Lord your shepherd refresh you in your daily places, stand beside you in your dark places, provide for you in your dangerous places, and welcome you into His dwelling places. Amen.

24th July '16

40

Now the God of Peace who brought up from the dead the great Shepherd of the sheep in the blood of an eternal covenant, even our Lord Jesus. May He equip you with everything good in order to do His will, doing in us what pleases Him. Glory is His into the ages and the ages. Amen.

11th September '16

41

Now may the Lord who hears your cry when your heart is faint continue to be the rock beneath you, the shelter above you, and the strong tower around you until Jesus comes. Amen.

25th September '16

42

Now may the God for whom you wait, lift you up out of the slimy pit, out of the mud and mire and set your feet upon a rock, and may He place you in the shadow of His wings until the storms of destruction pass by. Amen.

2nd October '16

43

Congregation of the Lord Jesus Christ, in all your darkness and troubles, remember what you are and have. You've been loved with an everlasting love, you are supported by everlasting arms, you are recipients of everlasting life, and heirs of an everlasting kingdom all sealed and made sure by the blood of an everlasting covenant. Amen.

6th November '16

44

God be with you till we meet again
By His counsel's guide, uphold you,
With His sheep securely fold you:
God be with you till we meet again.

God be with you till we meet again;
When life's perils thick confound you,
Put His arms unfailing 'round you
God be with you till we meet again. Amen.

22nd January '17

45

Now may God be your exceeding joy, Christ your only hope, the Holy Spirit your unfailing comforter in all your worship, in all your work, in all your troubles until Jesus comes. Amen.

5th March '17

46

Now may the Keeper of Israel keep you. May God our Father keep you from stumbling. May the Son of God keep you near the cross. May the Spirit of God keep you from idols. Amen.

19th March '17

47

The Shepherd who has laid down His life for the sheep, who calls you by name, who never abandons His flock or allows His sheep to perish, preserve you in all the attacks of the enemy, hold you steady in all your sorrows, and keep you faithful in all your temptations. Amen.

26th March '17

48

Now may the good Shepherd, who laid down His life for His sheep, continue to be your faithful Shepherd who defends you from all evil, who delivers you from all fear, who protects you from your own folly, who carries you home at last with rejoicing. Amen.

14th May '17

49

Now the companionship of the man of sorrows, and the power of the King of Glory, rest upon you all. Amen.

6th August '17

50

Now may Yahweh, the everlasting God, the Creator of the ends of the earth, who never faints or grows weary, may this God increase and renew your strength so that you can go on walking faithfully, whether in the light or in darkness. Amen.

1st October '17

51

The Lord is faithful who will strengthen you and keep you from the evil one. Now may the Lord direct your hearts into the love God has for you and into the steadfastness Christ gives you.

3rd December '17

52

Now to the One who keeps on loving us and who has set us free from our sins at the cost of His blood, glory and dominion belong to Him into the ages of the ages. Amen.

14th January '18

53

May this giving God give you wisdom in your perplexities, relief in your pressures, steadiness in your troubles, and faithfulness in your temptations until Jesus comes. Amen.

28th January '18

54

The goodness and generosity of God our Savior, the renewing power of the Holy Spirit, and the certain hope purchased by Jesus Christ settle over your living, your thinking, your worship, and your dying. Amen.

4th March '18

55

May the Word of God dwell in you richly in all wisdom to capture your hearts for Christ, to comfort your hearts in Christ and to humble your hearts before Christ. Amen.

18th February '18

56

Now may the God who did not even hold back His very own Son but handed Him over for us all, provide you with every good thing you need in order to do His will and do in you what pleases Him. Amen.

11th March '18

57

The Savior who is tempted in every way as we are, yet without sin, make you steady in trials, faithful in temptations, content with providence, and hopeful in troubles. Amen.

8th April '18

58

Now may the Savior, who has abolished death, come to you in your sorrows, stay by your side in the darkness, carry you through your distresses, and give you joy in the morning.

6th May '18

Afterword

I occasionally 'attend' an 11.00 pm Sunday evening service—*yes, p.m.*! I switch on the iPad, click on an app, and through the wonders of modern technology find a seat somewhere in a full church four thousand miles and five hours time difference away. For an hour and more I participate in the 6.00 pm evening service of First Presbyterian Church, Columbia, South Carolina and share in a service of worship, with heart-felt praise and prayer. Dr. Dale Ralph Davis is usually preaching, frequently from the Old Testament. It is a privilege to be 'there'. Then, sometime after midnight, I close down my iPad with the words of Ralph Davis's closing benediction ringing in my ears.

The pages you have just read contain many of these benedictions. I feel sure you will want to re-read them. As you do, imagine that you are there in the full congregation. You have just listened to Dr. Davis preach in a way that gives you confidence in the careful study and preparation that lies behind his exposition (he has been reading from his Hebrew Bible and translating on the spot). The message has been marked by great lucidity, with illustrations that illuminate, and with application that is clear, relevant, and at times very pointed and searching. In addition, you feel you have witnessed an illustration of Paul's words, 'We were ready to share with you not only the gospel of God but also our very own selves, because you had become very dear to us' (1 Thess. 2:8).

The service has been a benediction to you. The sermon has both instructed and nourished you. But as the final hymn comes to an end, there is one last word of gospel grace—as he pronounces the benediction Ralph Davis is as much preaching God's word to you now as he was in the sermon. He is not only praying for you; he is announcing to you all that is yours by faith in Christ. What a way to end the Lord's Day and to begin the week. You will have tasted some of that blessing in these benedictions. Would that every Christian congregation in the world knew such blessing!

But now the publication of this little book (without his knowledge!) marks Ralph and Barbara Davis's retirement from this ministry. I rank myself among those with most reason to be thankful to God for them, and to them for their faithfulness, for I love First Presbyterian Church in Columbia.

God seems to give pastors a love for their flock that is not so much a virtue they develop as a gift they receive, not something worked up from within but sent down from above, an 'I cannot help myself from loving them' kind of love. And so, they not only long to give their congregations their best but also for them to have the best. Even so, I do not think I could have dreamt that people I love dearly would ever have the amazing privilege of a ministry of the word that included hearing Dr. Derek Thomas on Wednesdays (at noon and at night) as well as on Sunday mornings, and then Dr. Dale Ralph Davis on Sunday evenings. This has been God's gracious gift. Now that season has come to a close. But God's benedictions last for ever. I know that Christians throughout the world are grateful for Ralph's many books of biblical exposition, and for the sermons which are today so accessible on the worldwide web. So, with many others I am glad that this little book of benedictions has omitted one so that all of us who appreciate and love Ralph and Barbara Davis can pronounce it on them in the name of Jesus Christ:

The LORD bless you and keep you;
the LORD make his face to shine upon you
and be gracious to you;
the LORD lift up his countenance upon you
and give you peace (Num. 6:24-26)

יְבָרֶכְךָ יהוה, וְיִשְׁמְרֶךָ

יָאֵר יהוה פָּנָיו אֵלֶיךָ, וִיחֻנֶּךָּ

יִשָּׂא יהוה פָּנָיו אֵלֶיךָ, וְיָשֵׂם לְךָ שָׁלוֹם

Sinclair B. Ferguson
May 2018

Also available from
Christian Focus Publications...

Robert Vasholz

BENEDICTIONS
A POCKET RESOURCE

ISBN 978-1-8455-0230-0

Benedictions

A Pocket Resource

Robert I. Vasholz

Benedictions are pronounced by ministers at the close of worship services as an expression of hope and encouragement to God's people to face whatever their future might hold. This makes them a Biblical norm for the end of worship—something we should consider doing each time we leave God's presence and go out into the world. If you are involved with leading worship in the church or in the home your next question will be 'Where do I go to find them?' Fortunately Robert Vasholz has done the legwork for you. He has collected in this one book the benedictions found in scripture along with some additional scripture enriched blessings for use during worship. Use them to help Christians have a greater effect on the world.

Robert I. Vasholz

CALLS TO WORSHIP
A POCKET RESOURCE

ISBN 978-1-8455-0338-3

Calls to Worship

A Pocket Resource

Robert I. Vasholz

In the common practice of Christian churches, across many traditions, a call to worship is typically a few lines of Scripture (or a combination of Scripture texts) expressed at the beginning of a church service. The call to worship exhorts God's people to turn from worldly distractions and to focus hearts, minds and actions on revering him.

If you are involved with leading worship in the church or in the home your next question will be 'Where do I go to find them?' Fortunately, Robert Vasholz has done the legwork for you in this book.

The first section is designed to address specific events common to the Church such as Christmas, Easter, etc. The second section pertains to calls to worship that ask for an audible response from God's people. The third part offers a number of calls to worship from the minister alone. It is my honest desire that this will serve as a proper and dignified way to enhance public corporate worship and to invite God's people to be attentive to the service that follows.

DALE RALPH DAVIS

THE WORD
BECAME FRESH

HOW TO PREACH FROM OLD TESTAMENT NARRATIVE TEXTS

ISBN 978-1-8455-0192-1

The Word Became Fresh

How to Preach from Old Testament Narrative Texts

DALE RALPH DAVIS

'...I still believe that traditional Old Testament criticism has had the effect of killing the Old Testament for the Church. This little tome can hardly reverse that, but it is meant as an exercise in reading the Old Testament for fun and profit. As my mother-in-law used to say, 'It's different anyway.' And maybe it will help. Most of what I do in the following pages involves discussing examples of Old Testament narratives. I have tried to select examples from a broad range of possibilities. By the way, I assume that you have the biblical text handy in order to carry on your "Berean" work.'

Dale Ralph Davis

'There is no more gifted expositor of the Old Testament in our day than Ralph Davis. His book not only brings scholarly research to bear on the subject, but also reflects his many years of preaching week after week through the Old Testament. What a gift to the church to have such a fine book.'

Richard Pratt
President, Third Millennium Ministries, Orlando, Florida

Christian Focus Publications

Our mission statement –

STAYING FAITHFUL
In dependence upon God we seek to impact the world through literature faithful to His infallible Word, the Bible. Our aim is to ensure that the Lord Jesus Christ is presented as the only hope to obtain forgiveness of sin, live a useful life and look forward to heaven with Him.

Our books are published in four imprints:

CHRISTIAN FOCUS

Popular works including biographies, commentaries, basic doc-trine and Christian living.

CHRISTIAN HERITAGE

Books representing some of the best material from the rich heri-tage of the church.

MENTOR
Encouraging Christians to Think

Books written at a level suitable for Bible College and seminary students, pastors, and other serious readers. The imprint includes commentaries, doctrinal studies, examination of current issues and church history.

CF4•K
Because you're never too young to know Jesus

Children's books for quality Bible teaching and for all age groups: Sunday school curriculum, puzzle and activity books; personal and family devotional titles, biographies and inspirational stories – because you are never too young to know Jesus!

Christian Focus Publications Ltd,
Geanies House, Fearn, Ross-shire,
IV20 1TW, Scotland, United Kingdom.
www.christianfocus.com